Gruesome and Bloodsocks On Wheels

The ancient car made a dignified but slow progress down Wellington Street as Gruesome stopped to talk or wave to various acquaintances. One thing she soon discovered was that the car was extremely noisy. The windows rattled, the doors creaked, the engine rumbled and there was a strange clanking noise coming from the boot.

'Wicked,' said Leotard. 'It's like being on the ghost train.'

Jane Holiday

Gruesome and Bloodsocks On Wheels

Illustrated by Steven Appleby

Young Lions

For Yewa

Published in Young Lions 1988
8 Grafton Street, London W1X 3LA

Young Lions is an imprint of
the Children's Division, part of
the Collins Publishing Group

Text copyright © Jane Holiday 1988
Illustrations copyright © 1988 Steven Appleby

Printed in Great Britain by
William Collins Sons & Co. Ltd, Glasgow

1

It was spring.

Outside the front door of Augusta Vampire (otherwise known as Gruesome Gussie), a medley of purple, yellow and white crocuses bloomed in an upturned police-helmet.

'Come *on*, Bloodsocks,' Gruesome said impatiently. She tugged at the lead, causing Bloodsocks to lash his tail furiously. Enough to give a cat indigestion, being dragged out straight after his breakfast like that. He sat down defiantly on the pavement and began to scratch his bottom. Gruesome didn't take the slightest notice. After months of secret driving lessons, which even Leotard Jones next door knew nothing about, she had passed her test and now she was going to collect her very own second-hand car from Trumpington Car Mart. She had been able to afford to buy a second-hand car with the earnings she and Leotard and two London friends, Julian and Maria, had made from a record called 'The Skeleton Jump'. They had won first prize in a talent contest and had even appeared on 'Tops of the Pops'.

'There,' she said to Bloodsocks. 'Isn't it neat?'

'It' was a very old cream-coloured four-door Morris Minor 1000 with a jammed boot, the front driving window stuck permanently open, stained and sagging seats, no indicator and galloping rust. Gruesome thought it was blissful.

'And a finer little model you won't find anywhere at twice the price, madam,' said the salesman (ginger moustache, tight-fitting grey trousers and navy blazer) as the

sale was completed. 'Can't beat these old cars for stamina.'

As Gruesome took possession of the log book and keys and settled herself excitedly in the driving seat, Bloodsocks reluctantly climbed in on the other side. He hissed and spat as Gruesome did up his seat belt.

Leotard came dashing out to meet them as Gruesome drew up proudly outside the house.

'Hey, Grue, you never told me you could drive. That's why you've been sneaking off all the time.'

Bloodsocks, unbelted, leaped down from the car at full tilt and shot into the house.

'I like your hat,' said Gruesome.

Leotard was wearing a purple jogging suit, red trainers, shades and a bowler hat with a silver moon stuck on the side.

Gruesome told him how she had passed her test first time as Leotard followed her inside.

'You've got a new sofa as well,' he said.

'Had to, didn't I?' said Gruesome. 'You know my other

6

one went down to London when I moved. I bet it's still outside 94 Gorefull Road. This one turns into a bed. I got it at that second-hand place in Trumpington next to the video shop.' She brought in some nettleade and a plate of dog-biscuits.

'Wicked,' said Leotard, taking three biscuits and smearing them with chocolate paste. 'My favourite.' He bounced up and down on the battered-looking sofa.

'Help. Arrrrrgggggggggggghhhhhhhhhhhhhhhhh,' he shrieked as his head fell suddenly backwards and his legs shot out. The sofa had turned unexpectedly into a bed.

Wriggoletto, the grass snake, uncoiled herself from the lampshade to see what was happening. She rewound herself contentedly round Leotard's bowler hat. Blood-socks, who had been sulking behind the television, peered out to see what was going on.

'Come on then,' said Gruesome. 'Finish your nettleade and I'll take you for a quick spin.'

Bloodsocks leaped quickly into the back seat before he could be belted up and Leotard folded his legs in beside Gruesome.

The ancient car made a dignified but slow progress down Wellington Street as Gruesome stopped to talk or

wave to various acquaintances – old Mrs Thomas busy washing her doorstep as usual, Big Pete Hardisty, the gravedigger, the Patel twins and Mrs Musa. One thing Gruesome soon discovered as she drove along was that the car was extremely noisy. The windows rattled, the doors creaked, the engine rumbled and there was a strange clanking noise coming from the boot.

'Wicked,' said Leotard. 'It's like being on the ghost train.'

'It's great,' said Gruesome. 'I can go for trips without having to shut Bloodsocks up in a basket.'

Just as they were driving along the main Trumpington road towards Lower Barton, they were flagged down by a policeman.

'Can I see your licence, love?' he asked, peering through the half-open window. He recoiled slightly as Gruesome beamed at him, revealing highly-polished fangs.

Gruesome produced all her documents. The policeman gave these a brief look. 'Just wait there,' he said. He walked all round the car, looking at the tyres and kicking them. Leotard got out to see what he was doing.

'I'll just have a look in the boot,' said the policeman, but after a fierce struggle with it, in which he could neither open it fully nor shut it, he gave up.

'You need to get that boot seen to, love, and this window fixed. You'll get rising damp else.'

Bloodsocks simpered at him in his most revolting manner and his expression changed.

'Now then,' he said, 'what have we here?' He felt in his notebook pocket and found two squares of milk chocolate which Bloodsocks accepted graciously.

'Fine upstanding cat you've got there,' said the policeman as he waved them off.

'Upstanding,' said Leotard, roaring with laughter. 'He'll soon be too fat for his legs to support him.'

Bloodsocks sagged back resentfully on to the rear seat. What a nerve. Perhaps he was a *little* plumper than when he was a kitten but at least he had more sense than to go round in a bowler hat and sunglasses.

After a short and noisy ride, Gruesome parked the car outside the Kwikbuy Supermarket, leaving Bloodsocks in the car. In a few minutes she and Leotard returned with a big box of groceries. Leotard took a can of catfood and attacked the boot lock with it. To their great surprise it sprang open. As they stowed the box inside, Gruesome noticed an umbrella lying on the boot floor. It was made of maroon and white material with a curved wooden handle.

'That's funny,' she said. 'I'm sure that wasn't there before.'

'Could have been,' said Leotard. 'You've never opened the boot before.'

'It's certainly not mine, anyway,' Gruesome said.

As they parked in Wellington Street, Leotard's Mum, Mrs Jones, came out.

'*There* you are Leotard,' she said. 'Hey, you've never learned to drive, have you, Gruesome? Is that your car?

Ee, you're a dark horse. Could do with a spot of paint, couldn't it?'

Her husband stuck his head out of the window. (The Jones lived in the flat above Gruesome in the corner terraced house.)

'Jean. There's a telephone call for Gruesome. From London it is.'

Gruesome's heart sank.

Could it be the other vampires? But no, surely Leotard would never have given them his telephone number?

2

But it wasn't Uncle Batticoop, Hideous Hattie, Four-Fanged Francis, Hirudinea or Annelid on the telephone. It was their friend Maria.

'She's showing some work in an art gallery in Manchester,' Gruesome told Leotard. 'She's staying with me for a few days. She sends you a big kiss.'

'Yuk,' said Leotard, disappearing rapidly into the kitchen.

As she went downstairs to her own flat, Gruesome heard Mr Jones complaining to his wife about Leotard.

'You've not let him go round Trumpington dressed like that surely, Jean? He looks like the back end of a donkey.'

'Donkeys don't wear bowler hats,' said Mrs Jones, 'especially ones with stars on.'

The next day Gruesome went to meet Maria at Trumpington coach station.

'Gruesome! Bloodsocks!' Maria cried, leaping off the coach while the driver hurried round to open the boot. She was wearing a red cape over red cords and a black shirt. Long red earrings swung from her ears and a red butterfly brooch perched among her dreadlocks. She hugged and kissed Gruesome and then gave Bloodsocks a big cuddle and a chocolate sardine.

The coach driver heaved several large awkwardly-shaped packages out of the boot.

'That's mine as well,' said Maria, pointing to a striped cotton bag.

'Good thing I brought the car,' said Gruesome as they

11

heaved the paintings and collages into the back of the car because they wouldn't fit into the boot.

Bloodsocks crouched on the window since there wasn't room anywhere else, and stoically sucked his chocolate sardine until they reached Wellington Street.

Maria was delighted to sleep on the sofabed.

'It'll be a change from sleeping in mid-air,' she said. Gruesome remembered that Maria had always slept in a hammock when she lived at Gorefull Road.

After some ice-cream, Gruesome decided to make a batch of parsley scones while Maria set up her painting materials in the living-room and started working away on some cardboard boxes which had to be finished before she took her stuff to the art gallery.

Before long there was a knock at the front door.

'I bet that's Jean Jones from upstairs,' said Gruesome. 'Wanting to see who's staying with me.'

Sure enough, there was Mrs Jones on the doorstep.

'Just popped in,' she said. 'I haven't seen much of you since we came back from Majorca.' Mr Jones had taken them on an unexpected fortnight's holiday recently to make up for the disappointment over the new council flats. The Jones had been all ready to move in when there had been a terrible scandal over the building contracts. Now half the council members were in prison on remand and the twenty-storey block stood untenanted.

'You'll be able to get around more love, won't you,' she said, 'now you've got your car? Oh,' she stopped, 'I see you've got visitors.'

Gruesome introduced them.

'Enchanté, Madame,' said Maria, putting on her best French accent and kissing Mrs Jones on both cheeks.

'Er . . . charmed I'm sure,' said Mrs Jones. 'Call me Jean, ducks.'

Gruesome made some raspberry tea and offered her a parsley scone.

'Freshly-baked,' she said.

'Ta love,' said Mrs Jones. She'd long since become accustomed to the black dustbin-liners pinned at the windows and the milk bottles full of weeds and dead flowers on the window-sills. Even the many spiders, descendants of Hairietta, had ceased to disturb her. She watched in fascination as Maria began to work thick splotches of paint on to one of the cardboard boxes with the flat of Gruesome's bread knife.

'She's an artist,' explained Gruesome. 'All these,' she waved her hands at the packages stacked against the walls, 'are for an exhibition in Manchester.'

'Oh, an *artist*,' said Mrs Jones. 'I *see*.' She quickly finished her tea and scone and began to tiptoe to the door. 'I won't disturb her,' she whispered. 'I saw a programme about an artist once on the telly. He got all hot and bothered and cut off one of his ears. Just fancy. Tara then, love. Ee, those crocuses are coming up a fair treat, aren't they?'

News soon spread that Augusta Vampire (alias

13

Gruesome Gussie) had acquired a car and before long, many people who knew her and others who didn't, came round to look at it. There weren't many cars in Wellington Street.

'I hear you've become a Yuppie, Gruesome,' said Mr Todd, the butcher.

'Yuppies aren't unemployed,' said Gruesome, 'not unless they're royal.' She had long since given up hope of finding a job. Vampires weren't a favoured group in the job market although Uncle Batticoop and the rest had managed to get two, first a job in Dieppe and then one in television commercials, but the latter was only because of Gruesome's sudden fame in the shortlived group, 'Gruesome and the Gravebugs'.

Gruesome soon found however that there were disadvantages in becoming a car-owner. Since she didn't have to go to work in it, people assumed she was always available to do them a favour.

Old Mrs Thomas asked her to take her and Susie, her Scottie, to the vet because she had a sore ear. Gruesome didn't mind that because the vet was quite close, but after this, Mrs Thomas hailed her every time she wanted to go shopping, just as if she were a taxi-driver.

Mr Todd, whose car was in the garage being serviced, asked her if she could take his wife to and from the hairdresser's in Lower Barton. She kept Gruesome waiting half an hour and complained bitterly about the wind blowing through the driving window (which of course didn't shut) and spoiling her new hair-do.

'Looked just like a bird's nest anyway,' Gruesome told Leotard.

The Patel twins stopped her one day, because they'd just missed the bus into Hartford where there was a Sports Centre, so she agreed to take them there. Coming back she met Big Pete Hardisty, the gravedigger, who

asked if she could give him a lift to Trumpington churchyard as he was late for work.

'My bike's got a puncture,' he said, 'and there's a
funeral at one o'clock sharp. Can't have a corpse lying
around with nowhere to put it.'

Mrs Musa, who had fallen out with Gruesome over
Wuneye, Hideous Hattie's pet vulture, now greeted her
as an old friend and frequently asked her for a lift to the
Doh-See-Doh Dance Studios. This was bad enough but
on the way there she often remembered she needed a
pint of milk or a packet of tea and Gruesome had to stop
at a nearby shop while she dashed in.

The last straw came one morning when Gruesome
rushed out to buy some *Pussiesteaks*. Old Mrs Thomas
stopped her and asked to be taken to the electricity
showrooms so she could pay her electricity bill. Gruesome
helped her buckle her seat-belt and deposited Susie
carefully on the back seat.

'Smells a bit fusty in here,' she said to Gruesome. 'You
ought to get it spruced up a bit. It's very untidy.'

'It's not a taxi,' said Gruesome, braking sharply to avoid a maniac in a bread van. Wriggoletto crept up her arm and wound herself round her forehead. 'It suits me very well.'

'And Susie's very delicate, you know. She's used to things being nice and clean,' Mrs Thomas went on. 'That back seat's all dusty.'

Gruesome gritted her fangs and said nothing. Her expression and the uncurling Wriggoletto, who had decided to attach herself to the window, frightened an oncoming lorry driver so much he pulled off into a side street and decided to have a nap before finishing his journey. 'Must be overdoing it,' he said to himself. 'I'm seeing things.'

'Can't you do something about the noise?' Mrs Thomas asked. 'It's giving me a right headache.'

Thankfully Gruesome pulled up outside the Electricity Board, unbuckled Mrs Thomas and handed out Susie.

'Sorry I can't stop. I've got to buy Bloodsocks' breakfast,' she said, and drove off, leaving Mrs Thomas standing crossly on the pavement.

Stinking hellebore, thought Gruesome as she belted round the supermarket, she didn't even say 'Thank you'. Her temper was not improved when she came out to find she had run out of petrol. She left the car in the Kwikbuy car-park and took a bus. It was only when she reached home that she remembered that she had left not only the car but also Wriggoletto behind.

3

Gruesome awoke to the smell of kippers. She pushed Bloodsocks off her stomach and stumbled out of her coffin. She felt tired and out of sorts. She remembered all the lifts she'd had to give to people in the last few days which had resulted in her running out of petrol. Wriggoletto was still missing and no one knew where she was. The manager of the Kwikbuy supermarket had not taken kindly to enquiries about a roving snake and warned Gruesome of unpleasant consequences if Wriggoletto turned up in the shop and frightened his customers.

Gruesome had finally driven home crossly to find Maria playing the violin in the back yard and Bloodsocks cowering behind the television with his paws over his ears. It reminded him of those dreadful days in London when he'd had to eat all kinds of disgusting scraps. *And* he'd been forced to take part in that awful pop group as well. He went all over cat-pimples just thinking about it.

Gruesome sighed as she smeared her kippers with blackcurrant jam and peanut butter and poured herself some dandelion coffee.

'You mustn't give lifts to all these people,' said Maria. 'They got along all right before. You know you can't really afford a car on the dole.'

'No,' said Gruesome. 'I'm not going to use it for shopping any more. I was so proud of passing my test I wanted to drive all the time, but now I'll just use it for longer journeys like going to Manchester. I want to see your exhibition.'

'It's only a small gallery,' said Maria, 'but I need to take all my stuff in today and tell them how I want it set

up and so on. These masks,' she waved half a kipper at the transformed cornflake packets, 'have to be set out in a special order and I have one piece which has to be tacked to the floor.'

Leotard looked in later and said he'd like to see the exhibition too.

'When are you taking the stuff there?' he asked.

'Today,' said Maria. 'But there's no room in the car, I'm afraid.'

'OK, I'll stay and keep a look-out for Wriggoletto. She'll probably turn up sooner or later.'

'I hope so,' said Gruesome, 'but she could easily have been run over in the car-park. Can you keep an eye on Bloodsocks as well, Leo? There's some *Pussiesteaks* in the fridge and plenty of milk.'

Bloodsocks rubbed himself against Leotard's legs in token of his approval of this worthwhile task.

Leotard reeled from the sudden onslaught. "That cat is *huge*,' he said. 'I reckon he weighs nearly as much as I do. Can't you buy him some Diet *Pussiesteaks* or get him an exercise bicycle?'

'Festering fungi,' said Gruesome, suddenly catching sight of the umbrella lying on the sofabed. 'I ought to do something about that. It must belong to the previous owner. I'll go along to the garage some time.'

She helped Maria arrange some of her works in the boot and stacked the others against the back seat.

Bloodsocks watched gloomily from the front door. Maria spelt trouble, he thought. She didn't get round *him* with her chocolate sardines. He padded heavily back inside, sniffed the umbrella carefully from all angles – there was something very faintly familiar and disturbing about it – and then settled himself on the sofa on top of Maria's black cotton pyjamas.

The ride to Manchester was uneventful, apart from Gruesome almost running over a slow-moving greyhound in a back street. The owner, an old man in a cap and ancient corduroys, shouted at her as the car rattled to a halt, 'That's a prize greyhound, that is! You should look where you're going.'

'Greyhound?' shouted back Maria. 'I've seen faster tortoises. *Espèce de cochon.*'

The man shook a gnarled fist at them.

'Lots of traffic,' said Gruesome as they lurched into the city. 'Is there something on?'

'Not that I know of,' shrugged Maria.

It was almost impossible to find anywhere to park until Maria remembered a friend of hers who lived a few streets from the gallery. Gruesome tooted the horn as instructed and a grey-haired woman leaned out of a third floor window.

'It's me,' shouted Maria. '*Bonjour Madame.*'

A conversation, completely incomprehensible to Gruesome, who knew only a few words of French, ensued and then Maria said, 'It's OK. We can leave it here.'

'Thank you,' Gruesome called up.

'My old piano teacher,' said Maria as they heaved everything out of the car. 'Now this is the difficult bit. Lugging everything from here to Mandela Avenue.'

It took them three journeys because Maria's works were not easily portable.

'Black Art Sisters Gallery', said a large black and gold board on the pavement outside a building sandwiched between a newsagent's and a vegetarian restaurant. A poster in the window proclaimed: 'Six Women Artists: New Exhibition in Mixed Media'.

After pressing the bell, Maria spoke into the entryphone and they were admitted. Someone called Amina dressed in a long silk tunic and matching trousers took them through the large L-shaped exhibition room into a kitchen where they met Tonu, a Nigerian woman who was wearing a blue sweater, jeans and very high-heeled sandals. She made them all some decaffeinated coffee.

Maria explained where and how she wanted her work displayed and then they went.

'Let's have something to eat next door,' she said. 'Not as interesting as your food, Grue, but it's not full of sugar and dangerous drugs or anything.'

Over broccoli quiche and chick pea salad Maria expounded her views on art and artists to Gruesome, with much waving of hands and forks. Gruesome nodded from

20

time to time, her mind running on Wriggoletto, the mysterious umbrella, and whether it had been such a good idea to buy a car.

'I'll pay you for the petrol,' said Maria, 'for both trips. I know you haven't got any more money than I have.'

'No,' said Gruesome. 'I've got a much better idea. Why not paint my car instead? Not with slogans,' she added hastily, looking at the badges pinned down the sides of Maria's trousers. 'Like a mural, only on a car.'

'Great,' said Maria. 'I'd love to.' She tore off a piece of the menu and began sketching out ideas on the back.

They walked back to pick up the car, tooting thanks to Maria's piano teacher before they left. Outside Piccadilly Station Gruesome noticed a large poster. She braked suddenly, narrowly missing a taxi.

'What's up?' asked Maria, as Gruesome took her by the hand and dragged her towards the poster.

'Would you believe it?' said Gruesome. 'That's why there are so many people about.'

Maria looked closely at the poster.

'GUEST APPEARANCE' it said in strident orange Dayglo letters, 'to open the magnificent refurbished eatery on Platform 6, UNCLE BATTICOOP and the VAMPIRES (as seen on TV ads).'

'*Incroyable,*' said Maria.

Gruesome hurried back to the car, hoping she wouldn't come across any of them before they were home in Trumpington. But no . . . there, perched on the bonnet of her ancient Morris Minor and looking for once remarkably kempt, sat Wuneye.

4

'How did you know this was *my* car?' demanded Gruesome. 'I've only had it a week.'

Wuneye flapped his wings and preened himself in the wing mirror.

'Quick,' said Maria, 'let's go before the batties arrive.'

'It's no good,' said Gruesome dismally. 'He'll only follow me to Trumpington and then Bloodsocks will have 99 purple fits. He can't stand Wuneye or the vampires, especially since Hideous Hattie fell on top of him and bruised his tail. And everywhere that Wuneye goes, the vampires are sure to follow.'

'Too late anyway,' said Maria. 'Look.'

Gruesome watched resignedly as she saw Uncle Batticoop, Four-Fanged Francis, Hideous Hattie, Hirudinea and Annelid bearing down upon them.

'Good of you to come and see us Augusta,' boomed Uncle Batticoop. 'No, don't be afraid,' he said, 'just because we've become celebrities. We're the same humble and charming vampires you've always known.'

To prove it, Four-Fanged Francis sidled over and gave her a nasty nip. Quick as a dragonfly, Maria banged him on the head with her mock crocodile handbag. Hideous Hattie sniffed and Wuneye immediately flapped over and balanced on top of her head.

'What are you doing awake at this hour anyway and how did you get up to Manchester?' asked Gruesome.

'Your appearance certainly hasn't improved, Augusta,' said Uncle Batticoop, looking at her long floral dress and her pink hair (dyed only the day before by Leotard). 'You always were wilful and wild. And always picking up

unsuitable companions,' he added, looking with disgust at Maria.

'Wilful and wild,' smirked Four-Fanged Francis, now at a safe distance from the handbag. He spat into a patch of oil.

'We had blood injections,' said Hirudinea, 'to keep us awake.' She twisted her bony hands in her stringy matted hair.

'Came by special jet,' said Annelid, eating a woodlouse with great relish.

Uncle Batticoop took off his hat and began treading on it and the other vampires shut up at once.

'Of course you know, we're famous now,' he said. 'That's why we were asked to open this new café.'

'Eatery,' corrected Four-Fanged Francis. Uncle Batticoop snapped at a passing bluebottle (which had no business to be about in May anyway) and swallowed it triumphantly.

'We forgot to let you know we would be here,' continued Uncle Batticoop, 'but obviously you found out about it.'

'I didn't know anything about it,' said Gruesome. 'If I had, I should never have come.'

There was an outbreak of tuttings and hissings from the assembled vampires.

'Jealous,' seethed Hideous Hattie, clutching at Wuneye's scraggy right foot. Wuneye, startled, toppled over and fell on to the bonnet of the car, knocking himself out.

'Too right!' said Maria, and amid mutterings of 'viper in my bosom,' 'comes of living with humans,' 'delinquent streak in her,' all directed at poor Gruesome, she produced a miniature bottle of brandy. Prising open Wuneye's beak, she poured the contents down his throat.

Hideous Hattie advanced towards Gruesome threateningly.

'If your *friend* has poisoned Wuneye, I'll . . . I'll . . . suck every drop of blood out of her body.'

Four-Fanged Francis hissed menacingly but kept at a safe distance from the mock croc. As if by magic, Wuneye opened his one good eye, lurched to his feet, uttering strange cries which sounded almost like singing, and set off in a swaying erratic flight away from the station over the Manchester rooftops.

'Poisoned, indeed,' said Maria. 'That was best brandy, that was.'

'Come back, come back, my darling doodums,' wailed Hideous Hattie as Wuneye disappeared from view.

'I blame you for this, Augusta,' said Uncle Batticoop sternly. 'You always had an unsettling influence. I dread to think what will become of you.'

'There's gratitude,' flared Gruesome. 'Who got you the advertising job in the first place?'

All five vampires looked at her with contempt and turned away.

Gruesome and Maria took the opportunity to scramble into the car and drive off at full speed (which wasn't very fast). The vampires, aghast at this latest proof of unvampire-like conduct, could only leap out of the way and throw curses and gravebugs after her.

5

'They had blood-injections,' said Gruesome later when they were safely back in Trumpington, 'to keep them awake. Fancy thinking I came to see *them*.'

'Don't bother about them,' said Leotard. (Maria was outside painting the Morris Minor as she had promised.)

'I'm not,' said Gruesome. 'It's that idiotic bird. Completely drunk he was. You should have seen the way he was flying. If he's charged with drunken flying, he'll probably end up back here. Talk about homing pigeons! Wuneye's a homing vulture, I reckon.'

'Except this isn't his home,' said Leotard.

Bloodsocks had begun to hiss when Wuneye's name was mentioned so Gruesome gave him a whole pot of cream with a teaspoon of honey in it as a special treat.

'By the way,' said Leotard, 'someone came round about some charity or other to do with cats. They suggested Bloodsocks should go on a sponsored walk for it.'

'A sponsored walk? Bloodsocks?' said Gruesome chuckling. 'You might as well ask a hyena to sing.'

Bloodsocks stood up with dignity. He wasn't that fat, for heaven's sake. Why couldn't he decide for himself?

'She's coming back tomorrow with some forms,' said Leotard, 'so you can decide then. It's for a good cause. Daisy Pratt's ginger tom's taking part.'

Bloodsocks padded off to the back yard where he flexed his paws and began pacing round the weed-infested flagstones. *Now was the spring of his discontent*, he thought miserably.

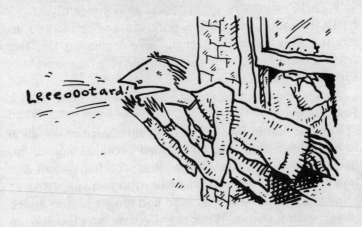

Leeeooootard!

Upstairs in the Jones' flat, Leotard's Mum was answering the telephone.

'Who?' she said. 'I'm afraid you've got the wrong . . . half a mo . . . hang on . . . is she that artist friend of Gruesome's? Right, I'll get her. Someone from Manchester for that artist friend of Gruesome's,' she told her husband.

'I hope this isn't becoming a habit,' he grumbled. 'We'll have people ringing up night and day if you're not careful.'

'Nonsense,' said Mrs Jones. 'It's not doing any harm. Nice young thing she is.'

She hung out of the window.

'Leeeeeeoooooooooooooooooootard,' she bellowed in a voice that could have been heard in Lower Barton. 'Phone call for that artist friend of Gruesome's.'

Maria was up the stairs in the flick of an eyelid.

'Thank goodness,' she said as she put the receiver down half a minute later. 'My friends in Manchester have found Wriggoletto. Thank you so much for letting me use your phone,' she said to Mrs Jones, giving her a hug and a kiss. Then she kissed the breakfasting Mr Jones on both cheeks and vanished downstairs.

'French,' said Mrs Jones, nodding significantly at her husband who sat amazed, a pork sausage halfway to his mouth. 'Her mother's French.' She'd gleaned this fact from Leotard the day before. 'Lovely manners the French, so friendly.'

'Yeah,' said her husband. 'Could teach that pillock Ron summat.'

Ron, his son-in-law, was a constant source of irritation to him. It was Ron who had helped Leotard shave all his hair off some time ago. It was Ron who had shown him how to paint his face. It was Ron who had suggested he grow a pigtail. It was Ron who had taught him to 'muck about' with a guitar. Whenever Leotard was involved in what Mr Jones called 'plain daftery', he could always be sure Ron had something to do with it. 'Not right in the head he isn't, that Ron,' he always concluded, whenever he talked about him to his wife. 'Don't know what our Bet sees in him.'

Downstairs Gruesome was puzzling over how Wriggoletto had infiltrated one of Maria's packets entirely unseen.

'She must have stayed in there all the way to Manchester and then popped up in the gallery,' suggested Maria, flopping down on the sofa.

'Aaaaaarrrrjjjjjjjjjjkkkkkkkkkkkq,' she screamed as it turned into a bed.

'Eeeeeeeeeeekkkkkkkkkkkkkkkkkkkkkkkkw,' screeched Leotard, who had been lying on the floor just behind and was now crushed beneath it. Maria was laughing so much she couldn't get up and Gruesome had to haul her off a somewhat squashed Leotard.

'You . . . you . . . bulldozer,' he shouted at Maria. 'I could have been smashed as flat as a pancake. You ought to look what you're doing.'

'*Mon petit chou*,' cooed Maria, rushing over to him. 'I

didn't know it was going to turn into a bed. There must be something wrong with it.'

Leotard fended her off but consented to her making him a soothing drink of hot chocolate. He sat down beneath Gruesome's skeleton collage and ate six dog biscuits and three parsley scones.

'What time are we going to Manchester tomorrow then?' he asked when he felt sufficiently soothed, picking up the umbrella and feeling its smooth wooden handle.

'About one o'clock. Have your lunch first,' Gruesome said. 'Maria says she'll finish painting the car today and then it can dry overnight. I'll have to take Bloodsocks. I don't like leaving him on his own. He gets really angry.'

But Bloodsocks, busy doing exercises in the back yard, had other plans.

'I just hope those vampires have gone back to London by then,' Gruesome said. 'I didn't realize they were getting so famous, but I suppose I haven't watched television lately.'

'Haven't you seen their latest ad,' said Leotard, 'for British Airways?'

advertisement:

GIVE YOUR WINGS A REST —
FLY BRITISH AIRWAYS

'British Airways?' said Gruesome in astonishment.

'Right. It has this slogan: "Give your wings a rest. Fly British Airways." Then you see these bat shapes flying down and turning into Uncle Batty and Co. It shows them sitting down in the first class with the stewardess serving them drinks.'

'Stinking hellebore,' said Gruesome. 'No wonder they're getting so pleased with themselves. They must be stuffed full of steak.'

'Perhaps they'll get free tickets to America like Joan Collins,' Leotard said.

'I hope so. I'm fed up to the back fangs with them,' said Gruesome. The whole Atlantic Ocean between us. Marvellous. Just look at the nip Four-Fanged Francis gave me this morning.' She showed Leotard a black mark on her chin.

'Not to worry. I'll paint something on it. No one'll notice. Anyway, what's it matter? You don't usually fuss about your face.'

'No,' said Gruesome, 'but it's the preview of Maria's exhibition tomorrow. There might be loads of people there. There'll be plenty of snacks,' she added as she saw Leotard's face drop.

'I hope they're not all like Maria,' said Leotard, 'or I shall wear a spacesuit. I don't hold with all this kissing and stuff. It gives me the freezing winjers. See you, Grue. I'll come round and paint your face tomorrow before we go.'

Gruesome went for a quiet lie-down on the flagstones in the back yard. She found Bloodsocks panting and looking extremely hot, lying on the dustbin.

'Are you all right?' asked Gruesome, feeling his forehead which was very damp. Bloodsocks uttered a feeble groan. His heart was thumping so loudly it was deafening him.

'Poor Bloodsocks,' said Gruesome. 'Let me carry you inside. You need a good rest.' She lifted him up, staggering a little, and laid him on a cushion in the living-room. Then she brought him some water to drink and bathed his forehead with a damp cloth. Bloodsocks relaxed and began to purr contentedly. Life wasn't so bad after all. It was a pity that poet chap was dead. He might have written a poem about *him* instead of MacCavity and Skimbleshanks. Never mind. He might get into the Guinness Book of Records if he kept on trying. With that satisfying thought he fell asleep and didn't stir all night, not even when Gruesome retired to her coffin. He had earned a night's repose.

6

The next day Gruesome was surprised to find that Bloodsocks most emphatically did not want to go with them to Manchester.

'I hope he's not sickening for something,' she said to Leotard.

'No, he's just sickening,' he said. He was wearing a pearl earring and had his pigtail looped over his head with the end of it fringed across his forehead. He wore baggy beige trousers, a cream grandad shirt, an olive green sweater and dark green plimsolls which he'd dyed himself.

Gruesome was wearing a long-sleeved loose green dress made from an old curtain of Mrs Jones', green canvas boots and a green necklace she'd bought from an Oxfam shop.

Leotard painted her cheeks, forehead, nose and chin with apples, bananas and oranges and painted her fangs pale green to match her dress. Maria was delighted with their appearance and had kissed both of them heartily before Leotard had time to protest. Then she made them all a huge omelette filled with sliced onions and treacle and a pot of garlic tea.

'I must go back to London tonight,' she said. 'But the exhibition goes on for three weeks so I'll have to come up again and collect my work. Who knows? Perhaps someone'll buy one of them.'

'Remember we have to bring Wriggoletto back with us,' said Gruesome. 'Perhaps we could bring a basket for him so he won't get lost.'

Gruesome suddenly remembered her car and dashed outside.

'That's absolutely brilliant,' she said as she saw how Maria had transformed what had been a rather down-at-heel Morris Minor into a work of art.

She'd painted the four seasons of the year. On the bonnet was spring; delicate pink-and-white blossoms of apple and cherry trees brightening up an urban street, patches of spring flowers in small front gardens and tiny green lawns, a magnolia tree. On the left hand side was summer; people in T-shirts, bright shorts and flowery skirts thronged a busy market, a bright sun, ice-cream vans doing a brisk trade to a queue of children. On the boot was autumn; children muffled in thick coats scuffed through tawny orange, red and brown leaves or gathered horse-chestnuts on their way to school, while shoppers battled to keep their umbrellas upright. On the right hand side was winter; on the front door was an indoor scene, a Christmas tree bedecked with shiny parcels and tinsel, and on the rear door an outdoor snow scene; children, hatted, booted and gloved made snowmen in scraps of gardens or slid down a nearby slope on trays.

'It's gorgeous,' said Gruesome to Maria. 'You've got so many details in it. I'm glad they're all townscapes.'

'Bloodsocks is on it somewhere,' said Maria, looking pleased. 'There, look, near the Christmas tree.'

'And there's Wriggoletto,' said Leotard, pointing to the summer market scene where she could be seen coiled round the post of a stall.

Gruesome was so delighted she gave Maria a big hug.

'Hey, you're getting as bad as she is,' said Leotard, quickly getting into the back of the car out of reach, and fitting himself round Maria's pictures.

'I must do something about that umbrella,' said Gruesome. 'It'll have to wait until tomorrow now.'

'I wonder how Marcus is getting on,' said Leotard as

Maria climbed into the front beside Gruesome and did up her seat belt. (Marcus was a frog who had gone down to London with Gruesome and Leotard and had then stayed behind there, taking up residence in the bathroom.)

'Flourishing when I last saw him,' said Maria. 'I went back there for some gear, after I'd moved into that other squat. The vampires don't disturb him at all. They sleep in the garden or on Grue's old sofa.'

Mrs Jones came rushing out just as they were leaving and admired the newly-painted Morris.

'It's ever so good,' she said. 'Pity to drive it. It ought to go in a museum.' She beamed at Maria and handed her a basket.

'Just some sandwiches and suchlike in case you get hungry on the way. I know you artists have to keep your strength up. Tara love. Behave yourself, Leotard. See you.'

Bloodsocks watched from inside the house as the car chugged off down Wellington Street. Gruesome had agreed to leave him behind. The place to himself at last. Wonderful.

At the Black Art Sisters Gallery, few people had yet arrived so Maria was able to check that all her pieces were correctly assembled and placed. Leotard and Gruesome drifted round together while Maria talked to the other five artists and Amina and Tonu, the organizers.

The first thing they saw were the cornflake packets from which Maria had made a series of masks. These were arranged on a set of shelves against one wall.

'It seems poor Wriggoletto got trapped inside one of those,' said Gruesome. 'They found her when they were assembling them, after we'd left.'

Gruesome especially liked a ten foot long piece which stretched along the floor like a piece of carpet, entitled 'There aint no black in the Union Jack'.

'I like these etchings,' said Leotard. 'Really neat.

Maria's dead good, isn't she? I like her stuff better than the others.'

They each took a glass of sparkling wine and a samosa from a side table at the far end.

'Mum would be absolutely tonto if she knew I was drinking,' said Leotard. 'Our Ron gave me some Guinness once and she went berserk. This tastes a bit better but I'd rather have Coca Cola.'

'Me too,' said Gruesome, 'but these snacks are good.' A lot more people had come in and were standing in little groups around the paintings and sculptures, talking in loud voices.

Wriggoletto, who had been unsuccessfully restrained in the back room, wriggled through the keyhole and came writhing over to them. She happily twined herself round Gruesome's neck like an additional piece of jewellery. This attracted attention and Gruesome soon found herself the centre of an interested group, not sure whether she was a piece of living sculpture, a visitor or an artist. Gruesome proceeded to talk to them about Maria's work and Leotard, bored, took a tray and went round offering wine to everyone. At last people drifted away in little groups, but not before many red SOLD stickers had appeared on various works.

'I've sold two of mine,' said Maria. 'Would you believe it? I put £25 on those etchings and they've both sold. I didn't think anyone would pay that much for them.' The three of them (and Wriggoletto) sat on the pavement outside the gallery eating the sandwiches, cake and cold drinks which Mrs Jones had packed for them.

As they were about to set off, they found a piece of paper stuck to the windscreen.

'Love your car. Superb painting. Would you consider selling it to me? Will pay twice what you paid for it. Professor Acquah-Dansa.' A phone number was scribbled underneath.

'Never,' said Gruesome. 'I'll never sell it. What an idea.'

They set off cheerfully, first securing Wriggoletto in a pair of tights with only his head sticking out, and arrived home feeling very pleased with themselves.

'That was a brill cake your Mum cooked, Leotard,'

said Gruesome as they drew up in Wellington Street, eliciting amazed comments from those people who had not yet seen the rejuvenated Morris. Indeed it had attracted a great deal of comment, both favourable and otherwise, throughout the journey.

An angry-looking Bloodsocks practically fell upon Gruesome as she opened the door.

'What's up?' asked Gruesome as Bloodsocks, mewing loudly, trotted ahead of them down the passage and through the kitchen. He scratched at the back door.

As soon as she opened it Gruesome knew what the trouble was. On top of the dustbin, displaying none of his previous sleekness, and with what looked like a luggage label attached to his right leg, crouched Wuneye.

7

Gruesome woke up late the next morning with a headache. The flat seemed strangely quiet and empty. Maria had gone back to London, Wriggoletto had disappeared somewhere and Bloodsocks, usually a familiar and reassuring weight on her stomach, was nowhere to be seen. Then she remembered Wuneye.

The note tied to his right leg had told her that Uncle Batticoop and the other vampires had been given free tickets as part of their payment from British Airways and were going to the United States to make a film. Wuneye couldn't go because of quarantine regulations, so, because they couldn't find anyone really suitable and blood being thicker than Coca Cola, they were entrusting him to Gruesome who was, after all, one of the family, even if a renegade.

Gruesome had forgotten, when she had wished them to the other side of the Atlantic, that they couldn't take Wuneye. He might have managed to fly across the Channel when they were working in Dieppe, but the Atlantic was quite another bundle of feathers. She wondered who had written the letter for them, since none of the vampires could write. Indeed the thought of doing such a thing disgusted them. She sighed as she made herself a cheese shake. Of course they hadn't said how long they'd be gone or thought of giving her any money to feed Wuneye, whose appetite was *enormous*. She remembered all the trouble he'd caused the last time he came. She'd have to remember to keep him hidden from Mrs Musa.

She went through to pick up the post and found a

sponsorship form had been pushed through the door. 'Felines Anonymous,' it said, '*the only charity for alcoholic cats. Sponsor your cat to walk for this deserving cause.*'

Gruesome snorted and went through to give Bloodsocks his breakfast.

'Boggling beetles,' she said, peering through the window. There was Bloodsocks carefully jogging round the flags, stepping over nettles, abandoned bottles and rusting pieces of dismembered clocks. 'Bless his bloody socks. He wants to go in for it.'

She went back inside and filled in the details on the form, putting her name down as first sponsor. Then she unlocked Wuneye from the bathroom and gave him a packet of raw bacon for his breakfast. Wuneye flew off with it to the top of the fridge and tore the wrapper off with trembling talons.

'He's going to be a real problem,' Gruesome said to Leotard later on. 'I can't keep him locked up all the time.'

'He'll get put in a wildlife park or a zoo if he doesn't

watch out,' said Leotard. 'Just don't let Mrs Musa see him, that's all.'

'Poor Wuneye, he's really fed up,' said Gruesome. 'He and Hideous Hattie are very fond of each other.'

'They may not be gone long. I expect it's only a film for a commercial.'

'Ask your Mum if I can borrow her shopping trolley,' said Gruesome. 'I daren't leave him behind when I go shopping. Bloodsocks can't stand him. Oh, and by the way,' she said. 'Take this form and see if you can get some people to sponsor Bloodsocks on this walk. He's really keen. He's been practising in the back yard.'

'Great,' said Leotard. 'He could do with losing a stone or three.'

Left alone except for Wuneye, who lay in a dishevelled heap on a beanbag, she slumped back despondently on the sofa. The sofa of course capsized once again, leaving Gruesome flat on her back.

Wuneye opened his one good eye and made a feeble croaking sound.

'Stupid sofa,' Gruesome said furiously, kicking it hard as she struggled to her feet. 'It's better just leaving it as a bed.' She went outside and lay down on the flags which were deliciously damp after an early morning drizzle. Bloodsocks was resting on the wall.

I've spent so much money, thought Gruesome, *I can't afford petrol for the car till my next giro money comes. What if the vampires stay in America? Whatever shall I do with Wuneye then?*

Soothed by the dampness and the pleasant aroma of rotting vegetation, Gruesome fell asleep.

8

The next day it was raining heavily. As she stuffed Wuneye into Mrs Jones' trolley-bag, leaving only his head sticking out, she wondered if the owner of the umbrella was now looking for it. She made up her mind to take it down to the police station later on and let them deal with it. Outside the Kwikbuy Supermarket she pushed Wuneye's head right inside the trolley, leaving only a couple of inches of the top unzipped so he wouldn't suffocate. She rushed round as fast as she could, which was quite slow because of pushing the trolley and holding the wire basket. She paused for a while by the frozen-food cabinets, wondering what was the best and cheapest thing to get to satisfy Wuneye's voracious appetite.

If only he was an ostrich, she thought. *They're supposed to eat anything. He could eat up all that rubbish in the back yard.* She delved into the beefburgers when a tremendous scuffle broke out behind her. A small boy in a striped boiler-suit was screaming his head off while his mother, who had been peering into the cabinets on the other side of Gruesome, crossly tried to find out what had happened. Gruesome leapt sideways into a carefully-positioned pyramid of pineapple chunks ('Today's Special Offer') which, with an almighty bang, cascaded into the aisle. Legs were bruised, feet were stamped on, tempers frayed. In but a few seconds a mini-riot had developed with beefburgers, biscuits, cakes and jellies hurtling through the air. Gruesome quickly removed herself from the scene of the crime, receiving a nasty blow from a flying Dundee cake as she did so. She spotted Wuneye perched on a vast mound of recycled toilet-paper. ('Unbelievable Knock-Down Price') nonchalantly eating the Curly Wurly he had snatched from the little boy. Gruesome pounced on him, stuffed him back into the trolley-bag and zipped it up right to the top.

'If you suffocate, it's your own fault,' she hissed. 'Why can't you control yourself for ten minutes? Anyone would think you came from a deprived background.'

She raced to the checkout. Fortunately there was one vacant as many shoppers were happily watching the fighting in Aisle 4. She had just packed everything into a plastic carrier bag when she was approached by a dark-suited man whose lapel badge announced him to be the Assistant Manager.

'Would you mind showing me what you have in that trolley, madam?' he said, giving Gruesome a very nasty look.

'Yes, I would mind,' snapped Gruesome. 'It's none of your business.'

'Ho, isn't it? It is if there's stolen property in there. You're supposed to leave all bags in the trolley park.'

'How *dare* you accuse me of stealing?' said Gruesome. 'I've sustained a severe injury from a Dundee cake while quietly going about my lawful shopping and you have the pig-faced effrontery to accuse me of stealing!'

'In that case . . .'

'Oh . . . Wonkybones,' interrupted Gruesome, who just wanted to get home. She unzipped the trolley-bag. 'There you are then.' A surprised vulture, with, Gruesome noted thankfully, no traces of chocolate or wrapping-paper round his beak, stared beadily up at him.

43

'Caaaaaaaaaaawwwwwwwwwwwwwww,' he rasped.

'Satisfied?' asked Gruesome.

The Assistant Manager, dabbing a tissue to his fore-head, managed a faint apology, before tottering off to Aisle 4.

'I shall take my custom elsewhere in future,' declared Gruesome as she stalked out, breathing a sigh of relief as soon as she and the trolley were on the pavement. 'Shop-lifting indeed. Someone should have bashed *him* with a cake.'

A shortish man with gingery hair, wearing a checked suit, watched her as she strode off down the street pushing the trolley with the bag of shopping sitting on top of it. She looked round as she turned into Wellington Street and was surprised to see the same man not far behind her.

Inside the house Wriggoletto and Bloodsocks were both sleeping peacefully in the coffin. Gruesome let the protesting Wuneye out of the trolley. He flew round the living-room six times, squawking indignantly. She unpacked the shopping and flopped on to the floor in front of the television.

Bloodsocks and Wriggoletto woke up and came in to

join her. Wuneye at last settled on a bean bag and decided to watch the television too for want of anything to sink his talons into. Gruesome began to doze off until a mournful screech from Wuneye woke her up.

He was jumping up and down and beating his raggy wings together. Gruesome looked at the screen and there were Uncle Batticoop, Four-Fanged Francis, Hideous Hattie, Hirudinea and Annelid. She sat up.

'There was a disturbance on a British Airways flight in the early hours of this morning,' said the newsreader. 'The pilot refused to leave Manchester Airport until five passengers were removed. The five passengers were later identified as "Uncle Batticoop and the Vampires", who have appeared in many TV commercials. The trouble is thought to have occurred immediately prior to take-off when one of the vampires, known as Four-Fanged Francis, bit a stewardess. In an attempt to restrain him, the senior vampire of the party, Uncle Batticoop, tried to stun him with a bottle. Unfortunately he floored the man sitting behind him instead. In the ensuing fracas, two people required first aid and the stewardess was rushed to hospital for a rabies injection. The five vampires were taken into protective custody. In the House of Commons today . . .'

Gruesome switched the TV off.

Wuneye subsided on to the floor. There was a banging at the front door. It was Leotard.

'Did you see the news?'

'You bet,' said Gruesome. 'Typical, isn't it? As long as they don't stop here. They should have been put on a daytime flight, they'd have been asleep then.'

She was about to shut the door when Leotard said, 'D'you know that man over there? He's been looking over here for some time.'

It was the man Gruesome had seen outside the Kwik-buy supermarket. As they looked, he crossed the road and came towards them. Leotard retreated inside.

'Yes?' said Gruesome.

'You don't know me,' said the man.

'No I don't,' said Gruesome, 'and I don't want a shower *or* any double glazing.'

'No no,' said the man, quickly putting his foot in the rapidly-closing door. 'It's not that.'

'And I'm not a Jehovah's Witness.'

'I've come for my umbrella. You bought my old banger. I forgot I'd left it in the boot.'

Gruesome scowled when she heard his disparaging reference to her car.

'Lovely job you've made of it,' the man said, as if guessing her thoughts.

'What's your umbrella like?' she asked.

'It's a maroon-and-white one. It's made of cotton and it's got a curved wooden handle,' the man said.

'Just wait there a minute please,' said Gruesome, closing the door. She didn't like the man but he'd described the umbrella correctly so she had no reason not to give it to him. She snatched it off the sofabed.

'I didn't like him,' she said afterwards to Leotard.

'A definite baddie,' he agreed.

'Why d'you say that? I didn't mean he was a crook or anything.'

'Bet he is, though,' Leotard said. 'Just look at this.' He handed Gruesome a small brown envelope. She peered into it and then drew out . . . 'Diamonds,' she said. 'A diamond necklace.'

'Right,' said Leotard.

'But where did you get it?'

'Out of that umbrella. You know the wooden handle? I was fiddling about with it when you were at the shops and something clicked open. It had this little hideyhole in it and there it was. I bet it's stolen.'

'I suppose so,' said Gruesome. 'It's not likely anyone would keep their jewels in an umbrella. But why did you take it out?'

'We couldn't let him get away with it,' Leotard said, 'not when it's probably been stolen.'

Gruesome didn't like the sound of this. 'But when he finds it isn't there,' she said, 'he'll come back for it.'

'OK. If it's really his, he'll come back and ask for it,

won't he? But if he's stolen it, he won't want you to know about it.'

'Right,' said Gruesome. 'So he'll try to break in and *steal* it back.'

'Don't worry,' said Leotard. 'I've worked out what to do.'

Gruesome didn't see how he could have but she'd had a tiring day and had too many other things to worry about. Most important of all was what was going to happen to the vampires and how much longer would she have to put up with Wuneye? Bloodsocks and Wuneye, she'd noticed, had called a truce, but how long would it last? And how could she afford to pay for all their food and buy some petrol so they could all have a trip out to the seaside?

Bloodsocks snuggled up to her and licked her face and Wriggoletto coiled round her feet in a figure of eight.

'See you, Grue,' Leotard said as he heard his Mum's bellow resound the length and breadth of Wellington Street. 'Don't worry. You might win the pools.'

'I don't do the pools,' objected Gruesome.

'There you are then,' said Leotard. 'You've already saved yourself some money.'

9

No charges were to be made by the pilot, stewardess or any of the aeroplane passengers, Gruesome discovered the next day. From the news she learned that the five vampires had made a formal apology to all concerned.

I bet, thought Gruesome. *Catch Uncle Batticoop apologizing to anyone. Must have been their agent. Perhaps they won't go to America now.*

Wuneye was very twitchy, as if he knew something was wrong. He fluttered up and down in an ungainly manner, uttering harsh croaks. When Gruesome found he hadn't eaten any of his breakfast, she began to get worried.

Bloodsocks was speeding up his daily training programme and now did an early morning jog down the ginnel before breakfast. Gruesome mashed some extra minerals into his food to keep up his strength. He had started to lose some of his flabbiness and was becoming much more agile. He didn't stagger or lurch about any more.

Gruesome suddenly remembered the diamond necklace and wondered where Leotard had put it. *That man will never come back and ask for it*, she thought. She made up her mind not to go out all day and to make sure that a potential housebreaker could tell the house was occupied. She put on all the lights and switched on the radio and television. She had no faith in Leotard's sorting things out, whatever he said. After all, it wasn't his flat that might be broken into.

She had to go out in the end, to find something tempting for Wuneye. She called Leotard to stay in the flat just in case.

She noticed that no one stopped to ask her for a lift, although Mrs Thomas was setting out with a shopping-basket, Susie trotting obediently beside her. Gruesome felt she'd been a bit sharp the last time she'd seen her so she slowed down to offer her a lift.

'No thank you,' Mrs Thomas said firmly, looking askance at the Morris Minor's painted body. 'I'd feel like a circus act. Proper daft it looks.'

When Gruesome returned from the shops, Wuneye was huddled in the kitchen looking like a little old man.

'Look, Wuneye,' she said. 'I've bought you a lovely piece of fillet steak.'

But Wuneye just scrunched himself up even tighter and took absolutely no notice. Gruesome quickly put the steak in the fridge. She was already feeling sick at just touching it and seeing the blood. Silver spots were erupting all over her face and hands.

'Best leave him alone,' said Leotard. 'Nothing we can do.'

Wriggoletto coiled round Leotard's left leg and began exploring his pockets.

'I wanted to arrange a day out somewhere,' said Gruesome, 'but I can't with him like that. He's a horrible bird but I don't like to see him unhappy.'

'He's pining,' said Leotard. 'That's what it is. He looks on Hideous Hattie as his Mum. Just imagine having Wuneye for a son.'

'Better than having Four-Fanged Francis,' laughed Gruesome.

The day passed quietly except for another telephone call from Maria in London via the Jones.

Maria told her when she was coming up to collect the paintings and Gruesome told her about Wuneye. She would have liked to tell her about the umbrella and its contents but not with Mrs Jones possibly overhearing and getting cross with Leotard.

'When's she coming up again then?' asked Mrs Jones. 'I expect she's very busy painting and such. Ooh,' she said, peering at Gruesome, 'you're allergic again, aren't you? You look ever so sick. It's the tension of modern life, that's what it is. They had a programme about it on the telly the other night only I was so worried about our Bet's op I couldn't keep my mind on it.'

Gruesome then had to ask about Bet and heard all about her operation and a whole lot of other things she'd much rather have known nothing about.

She retired early to sleep that night. Her silver spots itched so much she smeared fresh yoghurt all over them. Wuneye had stayed in the kitchen all day, hardly moving an inch. Gruesome left a plate of food beside him and a jug of water and hoped there would be some good news about the vampires for him in the morning.

She fell into a deep sleep with Wriggoletto and a considerably lighter Bloodsocks on her stomach.

'Peace, perfect peace,' she sighed. 'Tomorrow is another day.'

10

Indeed it was but it certainly didn't turn out as she had expected. Perhaps the worst thing about it was that it started so *early*.

Gruesome had been dreaming happily when she was jolted awake by the sudden removal of the weight on top of her stomach. She sat up blearily and looked at the clock which she'd found on a rubbish dump.

A quarter past one.

She groaned.

Bloodsocks was standing in the middle of the floor, his fur standing on end, his ears erect and his tail curved into a question-mark. Wriggoletto was lying in a straight line (most unusual for her) hissing menacingly.

Gruesome leaped up and tiptoed to the door. Could she open it without creaking? As it happened, it didn't matter because just then Wuneye set up a terrible squawking from the kitchen.

Gruesome ran, followed by Bloodsocks and Wriggoletto. A man with his jacket over his head was crouching on the kitchen floor with Wuneye croaking horribly, standing guard over him. Wuneye's untouched food lay in a mess of broken china.

'Wuneye,' called Gruesome. 'It's all right. Come here.' She took some more fillet steak out of the fridge and put it on a plate for him. 'There's a good vulture,' she said. 'Well done.'

Wuneye, much invigorated by the fray, attacked it with vigour. Gruesome felt a new batch of silver spots popping out all over her like door bells. The man took his jacket

off and dusted himself down, while Bloodsocks and Wriggoletto watched him balefully. It was the umbrella man.

'Heavens above,' he said, looking from Wuneye dribbling bits of steak from his beak to the silver-spotted Gruesome. 'It's like a bleeding zoo!'

'How dare you come in here and wake us up in the middle of the night?' Gruesome snapped. Bloodsocks lashed his tail fiercely and looked ready to sink his teeth into the burglar's leg while Wriggoletto writhed very very slowly towards him across the tiles. The man inched back till he was pressed against the kitchen sink.

'And how did you get in? You . . . burglar,' said Gruesome.

'Only came back to get my property,' said the man sullenly, his eyes rolling as he tried to keep one eye on Bloodsocks and one on Wriggoletto. 'That's a dangerous bird, that is, you ought to keep it locked up.'

'What property?' asked Gruesome. 'I gave you your umbrella back, though what it was doing in my car, you never explained properly.'

'There was something *in* the umbrella,' said the man. '*That's* what I want back.'

'Huh,' scoffed Gruesome. 'How can you keep something in an umbrella? It'd drop out on your head when you put it up.'

'OK,' said the man menacingly. 'I know you've got the diamonds. If you won't hand them over quietly, I'll have to use force.' He put two fingers in his mouth and gave a loud whistle. Through the kitchen door (*did I forget to lock it last night*? wondered Gruesome) walked someone whom not only Gruesome but also Bloodsocks recognized.

It was a big burly man dressed in a Donald Duck sweatshirt and jeans.

'Bruiser Bates,' gasped Gruesome.

Bloodsocks spat and Gruesome quickly picked him up

before he could spring at the criminal, who was carrying a nasty-looking stick.

Bruiser Bates groaned when he saw them. 'Not you lot again,' he said. 'It was you who landed me in the nick last time.'

'Shut it,' said the umbrella man. 'Just hand over the diamonds or your dear little pussy-wussy,' (Bloodsocks snorted with fury) 'is going to get hurt.'

'I don't know where they are,' said Gruesome. 'Leotard . . .' she stopped. Suddenly there was Leotard peering under Bruiser's arm into the somewhat crowded kitchen.

'Can I help Grue?' he asked. 'Heard a bit of noise so I thought I'd see what was up.'

Bruiser Bates grabbed his arm. 'You as well,' he said. 'I might have known. Come on then, smartypants. Give us the diamonds.'

To Gruesome's horror, Leotard felt in his pocket and produced the brown envelope.

'There you are, all safe and sound. They're no good to us anyhow.'

The umbrella man's hand knocked Bruiser's burly mitt out of the way and closed like a vice upon the envelope.

'Right, Bates,' he said. 'Let's go. Not a word of this to anyone, mind,' he said to Gruesome, 'or that cat will be minced and made into shepherd's pie.'

The door slammed behind them.

'Leotard,' cried Gruesome. 'Why did you give them the diamonds?'

'Don't worry,' said Leotard. 'I phoned the police first. They're on their way.'

'But they won't be here in time. There'll be a getaway car.'

'Ah,' said Leotard. 'I've had my spies posted and the umbrella man's car is parked a couple of streets away. He didn't want anyone round here to see it.'

Leotard opened the kitchen door to show her and,

seizing the opportunity, Wuneye flew out of the door straight past them, dropping shreds of steak as he went. He zoomed full tilt down the ginnel.

'What's happening?' cried Leotard and raced off after him, followed by Gruesome. Bloodsocks went back to sleep. He had had sufficient exercise for one day.

At the top of the street it became clear why Wuneye had suddenly flown off in top gear. Approaching from the direction of Lower Barton were five bat shapes. Wuneye croaked hoarsely at them and they responded by swooping down and knocking Bruiser Bates and the umbrella man to the ground. They were still lying there, too terrified to move, when Leotard and Gruesome arrived on the scene. Several minutes passed before the police (one man on a bicycle) arrived.

'But . . . where's the panda?' asked Leotard.

'It's Saturday night,' said the policeman, whom they all recognized as P.C. Gartside. 'What d'you expect?'

They all ended up accompanying the two handcuffed men to the police station. The diamond necklace was on their list of stolen property and the umbrella man turned out to be well known to the police as 'Sneaky Sam'.

'Really, Bruiser,' said P.C. Gartside. 'Only just out of the nick and here you are in trouble again. Thanks, folks,' he said to the vampires. 'I believe you helped in his capture.'

'Yes,' said Leotard. 'Perhaps they should join the police force. At least they got there before you did.'

The reunion of Wuneye and Hideous Hattie was very touching. Wuneye sat on her head and flapped his wings round her face until Gruesome thought she would suffocate.

'I shall never leave you again, never, never my doodums,' cried Hideous Hattie, as they all returned to Wellington Street.

'I don't know how it is, Augusta,' said Uncle Batticoop,

'but there always seems to be a disturbance whenever you're about. Why can't you lead a quiet life like any self-respecting vampire?'

'Self-respecting vampire,' piped up Four-Fanged Francis.

Uncle Batticoop cuffed him on the head. 'And don't *you* dare say another word, after all the trouble you've caused. Still,' he sighed, 'I dare say it's your dreadful example, Gruesome, which has influenced him.'

Gruesome knew now what people meant when they said their blood was boiling. She could have had a Turkish bath in hers.

Hirudinea spat as if in confirmation of Uncle Batticoop's words and Annelid flicked several slimy wriggling gravebugs at her.

Gruesome showed them into the back yard and gave them a pile of steaks out of the freezer. There the five of them remained all night, making a fearful racket until dawn. Gruesome sank gratefully into her coffin.

'*Blow, blow, thou winter wind, thou art not so unkind as vampires' ingratitude*,' she muttered as she snuggled up to Bloodsocks and tried, in vain, to shut her ears to the noise of the vampires outside.

59

11

She didn't wake up till midday. All was as quiet as the grave in the back yard. The five vampires, sprawled out all over the flagstones, were not a pretty sight.

Bloodsocks decided to extend his early morning jog down Wellington Street now he was getting fitter. Leotard had already got twelve sponsors for him and hoped to get more. He came round about two o'clock.

'Wow! Your face, Gruesome! You've got spots the size of grapefruit.'

'I'm just one big spot,' said Gruesome, 'and I feel sick too.'

'Funny how the vampires got there just at the right time, wasn't it?' he said. 'Good thing, since the police were late.'

'They always are,' said Gruesome sourly. Her head ached and a drowsy numbness filled her senses.

'But you'll have to get shot of them quickly,' he said. 'My Mum was nagging on about them something awful. They made a fearful row all night. Worse than five ghetto-blasters.'

'Don't I know?' said Gruesome. 'I was nearer to it than you, you know. I hardly got a wink of sleep all night. Only Bloodsocks didn't turn a hair.'

Leotard watched admiringly as Bloodsocks returned from his jog and did a few quick press-ups before breakfast.

'That cat's changed,' he said. 'He's so sleek and fit. To think a few weeks ago he was so flabby he couldn't see his paws.'

'Yes,' said Gruesome. 'He was upset last night when

he saw Bruiser Bates again but he soon got over it.'
(Bloodsocks and several other animals had been kid-
napped by Bruiser a few years ago, not long after
Gruesome had first moved to Wellington Street.) 'But the
problem is, what's to be done with that lot out there?
From what they were saying they've decided not to go to
America after all. Hideous Hattie has sworn never to be
parted from Wuneye again.'

'That's a relief,' said Leotard.

Fortunately, the film-makers decided they could still
make the film without transporting the vampires to America and, luckily for them, their capture of Bruiser Bates
made up for their fall from grace in the aeroplane
incident.

According to the 'Daily Pancake', Uncle Batticoop had
apologized 'on behalf of the delinquent vampire, known
as Four-Fanged Francis,' who had been suffering from
'nervous tension as a result of overwork'. He had gone
on to say that 'the unfortunate influence of a relative also
could not be ruled out as a contributory factor,' and
through his agents, Supadoopa Productions Ltd of Regent

Street, he expressed regret 'for any injury or damage incurred, for which all involved would be fully compensated.'

'"Unfortunate influence of a relative",' sniffed Gruesome. 'He means me. I'll never speak to any of them again. *Nervous tension*, my big toe! Four-Fanged Francis doesn't have a nerve in his body.'

At half-past midnight, a chauffeured Daimler with tinted windows arrived to take the vampires back to London.

'They must be making a fortune,' said Gruesome as she thankfully watched them depart. 'Could buy themselves ten steaks a day if they wanted.'

Mrs Jones was also watching, no less thankfully, from an upstairs window. 'Thank goodness they've gone,' she said to her husband. 'Really lower the tone they do, especially that blessed vulture.'

Gruesome went happily to sleep that night knowing she would not be woken up by burglars or serenaded by the vampires' ghostly howlings.

At last it was time for the sponsored cat walk for Felines Anonymous. A large area of Trumpington Park had been cordoned off for the event. Many eager owners had assembled with their reluctant cats. The owners were allowed to walk round with their cats for the first two or three laps until the cats become accustomed to it.

'Daft really,' said one bystander. 'Cats hate being all crammed up together.'

This proved to be correct so it was decided that the cats would have to be taken round only two at a time, and then starting at opposite ends.

Very few of the cats, all shades from white through grey, tabby, ginger and tortoiseshell to black, showed much community spirit or social concern. Most of them dropped out after one or two laps. A Siamese, who was disgusted to find himself among such a common bunch,

defiantly sat down after taking only three minute steps and had to be removed, amidst jeers and boos, by his embarrassed owner.

Bloodsocks awaited his turn patiently. He too disliked the company of most other cats but he just tried to pretend they weren't there. From as far back as he could remember, he'd lived in churchyards with Gruesome until she had been evicted from Lower Barton Churchyard by the other vampires and had gone to live in a council flat.

When it was his turn, he padded round slowly, ignoring the ginger tom whom he passed on the other circuit, who was soon replaced by a tortoiseshell, two tabbies and a grey. Interest quickened and soon Bloodsocks was getting a cheer as he completed each lap. Every two laps, Gruesome offered him some glucose water and mashed sardine.

An hour later, he was in sole command of the field. All the other cats had long since departed with their disgruntled owners who demanded that Bloodsocks should be tested for drugs and looked at Gruesome very suspiciously. When Bloodsocks had completed thirty laps he

stopped, to loud applause. In response to many requests, Gruesome then carried him round on a lap of honour before driving him home in triumph.

'Bloodsocks, I don't know how you did it,' she said. 'You were amazing.'

Bloodsocks didn't hear. He was asleep.

12

Bloodsocks was so famous after this tremendous effort for charity that Gruesome was inundated with parcels, letters and presents for him. Once again Gruesome had to pose for photos with him for the 'Daily Pancake'. She was not at all surprised when the photograph was printed with the caption: '*Miss Angela Viper and her record-breaking cat, Bloodlust.*'

She had to stockpile in her bedroom much of the food and gifts. There were dozens of tins of catfood from all the leading petfood manufacturers, boxes of chocolates, tins of biscuits, fish of every kind from sardines to salmon, rice puddings, bottles of vitamins and minerals as well as a huge bag of organically-grown oatflakes. The fridge was full of cartons of cream, ice-cream, chocolate mousse and trifle.

This wasn't all. Admirers also sent ribbons, bows, bells, cat baskets, sweatbands, pedometers, clockwork mice and photographs of the Royal family. Bloodsocks became absolutely unbearable. He stalked about with his tail in the air and demanded three meals a day, which he would eat only from a special silver-plated dish sent from an admirer in Abergavenny. He had a stainless steel drinking-bowl for water and a Wedgwood bowl for milk which now had to be heated gently before he would drink it.

Someone else had sent a leather-backed brush and comb set for him and he expected Gruesome to groom him carefully every day. When he travelled in the car, he had a special cat basket with a silk cushion. He didn't sleep with Gruesome in her coffin any more but in a sheepskin-lined 'Pussieden'. ('Yuk,' said Leotard when

he heard.) He now ignored Wriggoletto, who started to lie in wait for him to trip him up.

'I wish he'd never gone in for that wretched walk,' grumbled Gruesome. 'It's turned his head. Everywhere we go, people stare at him and stroke him and stuff him full of chocolates and biscuits.'

'Nine days' wonder,' said Leotard. 'But if he keeps on eating at that rate he'll end up just as fat as he was before.'

'Right,' said Gruesome, 'plus he's completely given up jogging.'

'At least you don't have to buy him any food,' said Leotard.

'That's the one good thing,' said Gruesome. 'I must have been mad buying a car – I can't afford to run it. It's not only the petrol. I need a spare tyre too.'

Soon it was time for Maria to come up again and collect her paintings. Gruesome drove up to Manchester and they parked the car in the same place as before. This time it took only two journeys to and from the Black Art

Sisters Gallery as Maria found that two more pieces of work had been sold. When they returned to the car, they found Maria's ex-piano-teacher admiring it.

'You are lucky to own such a beautiful vehicle,' she said to Gruesome. 'I much admire your steering-wheel cover too – such a beautiful woven pattern.'

'That's no steering-wheel cover,' laughed Gruesome. 'That's my grass snake.'

Wriggoletto lifted her head and waved it to and fro.

'*Charmante*,' said the piano teacher.

Back at Wellington Street they found Bloodsocks gorging himself on a three-course meal of tinned salmon, pineapple chunks and cream, and chocolate mousse.

'Heavens, Gruesome! Why on earth has he got all these fancy bowls?' asked Maria. 'You're spoiling him. Give them all to a jumble sale.'

'But they were presents,' protested Gruesome.

'Maybe,' said Maria, 'but just look at him. He's not the friendly cat he was. He didn't even greet me when I came in.'

'He'll get over it,' said Gruesome, 'once people stop

68

making such a fuss of him. Now, where shall we go tomorrow for our day out?'

After a lot of discussion they finally decided on Fiddlepool as it wasn't too long a drive, Gruesome knew the way without using the motorway (which she hated) and there was plenty to do there.

'I just want to lie on the beach,' said Maria, 'as long as it doesn't rain. And maybe go for a swim.'

'I want to paddle,' said Gruesome, who had seen people doing this on films.

'And Leotard will want to play games,' said Maria. 'He's not into sitting still.'

They set off early next morning with baskets of food and cold drinks and a spare can of petrol. Bloodsocks decided grudgingly to come. He'd finished all the fresh food in the fridge and was working his way through the tins of food in the bedroom. He sat in a cat basket beside Leotard while Wriggoletto preferred to travel on the roof.

They enjoyed themselves in Fiddlepool. They found a good place to park. Gruesome paddled and collected lots of seaweeds. Maria lay in the sun and had a short swim. Leotard played beach-cricket with a family from Wigan. Bloodsocks dozed in the sun. Wriggoletto had a good time weaving in and out of the sand and popping suddenly out of people's sandcastles and giving them a fright. They all had plenty to eat. They also found time to look round the town, buy a present for Mrs Jones, take a boating trip on an artificial lake (except for Bloodsocks) and sample the funfair (Bloodsocks adored the candyfloss). It was a very hot day, there weren't too many people, and they all set off for home in a very cheerful frame of mind.

It was on the way home that things started to go wrong. First the front left tyre got a puncture. The others got out and pushed while Gruesome steered the car on to the grass verge.

'Thank goodness I didn't go on the motorway,' said

Gruesome. 'It would have been much worse.' Fortunately she had managed to buy a spare tyre and there was a jack and a few other tools in the boot. They took turns at trying to unscrew the wheel, but it was no use. Exhausted, they all subsided cross and dirty on to the grass.

'It's screwed up much too tight,' said Maria. '*Sacré bleu.*'

They kept on trying, getting crosser and crosser until at last they succeeded. It took them nearly as long to get the new tyre in place as it had taken to remove the old one. At last they were on their way again, just as it was starting to get dark. Gruesome enjoyed the breeze which blew through the car but Maria and Leotard complained of the cold. Neither of them had brought a cardigan or jumper. Then Maria grumbled that the clanking and rattling was giving her a headache. She hadn't noticed it going. Leotard said that the squeaking of the ill-fitting doors was making his teeth hurt. Then they both said they were hungry and it was discovered that they'd left all their remaining food and drink on Fiddlepool Beach.

After this, to everyone's consternation, Bloodsocks was sick all over the back seat *and* Leotard's trousers. Even when all this had been cleaned up, there was a very nasty smell in the car. Bloodsocks crouched in a corner on the floor and wouldn't look at anyone. Then of course it started to rain. Gruesome loved it but no one else did. Before she could work the windscreen wipers, she had to prise Wriggoletto off one of them. Usually the most good-tempered of snakes, she reacted to this with irritation and wriggled furiously round and round and round the inside of the car roof. At last Leotard tied two knots in her whereupon she hissed unceasingly until they arrived at Trumpington.

Maria and Leotard both had streaming colds the next day, although this didn't stop Maria catching the coach to London. Leotard however, was kept in bed for several days. Wriggoletto spent the entire day, after their day out, at the top of the drainpipe, ignoring anyone who approached her. The only good thing was that since his return Bloodsocks had stopped stalking about expecting to be waited on hand and paw. He was afraid that someone would mention his dreadful lapse of behaviour which still made his whiskers quiver whenever he thought about it. Even the news that he was to be included in the Guinness Book of Records didn't excite him. He abandoned his fancy cat basket (which Gruesome gave to the Oxfam shop) and went back to sleeping on Gruesome's stomach.

'You can't please everybody all of the time, Bloodsocks,' said Gruesome.

13

Gruesome came to several conclusions after the day out at the seaside. The most important was that she couldn't afford to run the car and, in any case, wasn't enjoying owning it as much as she'd hoped. She gave it a good wash-down inside and out, put a plastic cover over it (donated by Mr Todd) and decided to use it only on special occasions. She started walking to the shops again. At least Bloodsocks would get some exercise, now he'd given up his jogging. With all the extra food he'd been eating, he'd returned to his former size and showed every sign of reaching gargantuan proportions before long.

She also tried out some recipes using the seaweed she'd brought back from Fiddlepool and found that seaweed cutlets were her favourite. She started making a new collage out of shells, fishbones, dried weeds and prune stones. Then one day, looking through the pockets of a dress, she found the note Professor Acquah-Dansa had left on her car.

'Why not?' she thought. She went to the telephone booth at the end of Wellington Street. '999 calls only' it said. She tried six telephones and walked two and a half miles before she found one that worked.

She dialled the number on the paper.

'Hello?' said a cautious voice.

'Could I speak to Professor Acquah-Dansa, please?' said Gruesome nervously. She didn't like talking to people she didn't know.

'Who is that speaking, please?'

Why did he want to know, thought Gruesome. Would

the Professor only speak to certain people? She didn't like being asked her name.

'Who is that, please?'

'Er, Augusta Vampire,' she said at last.

'Sorry. Could you repeat that, please?'

'*Augusta Vampire*,' said Gruesome, who felt like spitting down the telephone by this time.

The receiver at the other end was put down abruptly.

Gruesome sighed and redialled.

'Could I speak to the Professor?' she asked again.

This time it was a different person.

'Who is it, please?'

'This is Augusta Vampire,' said Gruesome, speaking very slowly and distinctly.

She heard the person at the other end talking to someone else. Then the person who had first answered the phone to her came on the line again and said, 'Look honey, I know it's a laugh a minute but we're busy people. Go try your practical jokes some place else. Got it?' The receiver was banged down.

'Once more unto the breach, dear friends,' said Gruesome, 'as an old friend of Uncle Batticoop's once said.' She put her last 10p in the box.

'Who's speaking, please?'

'Hermione Higginbottom,' she replied.

'Hold the line, please.' Gruesome almost fainted with shock. She was actually going to be allowed to speak to the Professor.

The Professor was delighted when he realized what she was ringing up about. 'But that's grand,' he said. 'I want to take it back to the States with me.'

'It's very old . . .' Gruesome began doubtfully.

'Not to drive, you understand,' said the Professor happily. 'To put in my Museum. I have recently opened an amazing new Museum of Modern Culture in my home

town. I think your car would be a most suitable object for it. You must come and visit it, Miss Higginbottom.'

'Vampire,' said Gruesome.

The Professor babbled on until Gruesome managed to ask him how much he would pay. He named a price far beyond Gruesome's hopes and agreed to bring the money round that afternoon at three o'clock.

Sure enough, at three o'clock the Professor arrived in a taxi. He was a tall slim man wearing a cream safari suit, a floppy beige hat and ginger suede boots. A stripey canvas bag hung over his arm. He examined everything with great interest and tried to buy the flowering police helmet, the skeleton collage, Wriggoletto (who was now restored to her usual good humour) and Leotard's bowler hat which Gruesome was mending for him. Gruesome told him about Maria and gave him her address in case he wanted to buy anything from her, since he liked her painting so much. He asked so many questions and seemed to have such an insatiable curiosity about everything that Gruesome thought he would never go. At last

Gruesome stood up and said she had to take Bloodsocks for his afternoon walk and, after a final seaweed cutlet, he departed.

'Goodbye now,' he said. 'Have a nice day!'

14

'Fancy Gruesome selling that car,' said Mrs Jones some days later.

'Not really,' said her husband. 'Terrible old banger. She should never have bought it.'

'I expect she got bored. There's nowt to do in Trumpington when all's said and done.'

'Well, I think she's found something to do now. Look there.'

'Eh, where d'you mean?' Mrs Jones looked down into the street but all she could see was Bloodsocks sunning himself on the pavement and what looked like a brand-new motorbike speeding towards them. Flashes of its blue and silver body could be seen as it came to a stop . . . outside the house. The driver and passenger dismounted.

'That's *never* Gruesome,' cried Mrs Jones as she took in the long dress below the helmet.

'Who else would be wearing a motor-cycle helmet over a long flowered dress and plimsolls?' asked her husband.

'And that's our Leotard on the back!' exclaimed Mrs Jones as she watched her son removing his helmet. 'He never said.'

'It's all right, Jean. He's got good boots on and a brand-new helmet by the looks of it. He'll come to no harm. And it's a lot quieter than that heap she called a car.'

'Spectacular, isn't it?' said Gruesome as they unbuckled their helmets.

'Brill,' agreed Leotard.

'It's so windy and cold when you ride fast,' said Gruesome, 'even though it's a hot day. That car was just like a moving house.'

'And I can't see old Mrs Thomas or Mrs Musa wanting lifts to the shops on it,' said Leotard.

'Right,' said Gruesome. 'And Bloodsocks won't come near it. He'd as soon go in a rocket to the moon.'

'Quick,' said Leotard as he saw the Patel twins, Sam Musa, Sharon Greenhalgh and Darren Cooper from Enfield Street, and Yen Mac Hoa from the 'Lotus Garden' in Garpole Road all racing down the road towards them. 'I expect *they* all want a ride. Get inside.'

They dashed in and Leotard lounged on the sofabed which Gruesome had long since stopped trying to use as a sofa, whilst Gruesome brewed some parsnip tea.

'I should have got a Honda 125 in the first place,' said Gruesome. 'It's more my style. There's just one thing I'd like, though.'

'What's that?' asked Leotard.

'I'd just like the vampires to see me riding it,' said Gruesome. 'Can you imagine Uncle Batticoop's face when he sees me in a skid lid? He'll swallow his top hat.'

My Best Fiend
SHEILA LAVELLE

'My best friend is called Angela Mitchell and she lives in the house next door.' There is nothing unusual about this opening description Charlie Ellis gives of her best friend, but the tales that follow reveal the very unusual scrapes these two friends seem to get into.

Pretty Angela's marvellous ideas usually lead to disaster. Like the time they got stuck on a single-track railway bridge over the River Thames with the rattle of train wheels getting closer and closer; and the time Angela accidentally caught an escaped circus lion in the back garden. But when Angela suggested burning down her dad's garage so that he could claim the insurance for a new one, Charlie really thought things had gone a bit too far. For somehow it's always plainer Charlie who ends up taking the blame, and the spelling mistake in her English essay really wasn't much of a mistake at all.

Simon and the Witch
MARGARET STUART BARRY

Simon's friend the witch lives in a neat, semi-detached house with a television and a telephone, but she has never heard of Christmas or been to the seaside. However, she has a wand, which she loses, causing confusion at the local constabulary, and a mean-looking cat called George, who eats the furniture when she forgets to feed him. The witch shows Simon how to turn the school gardener into a frog, and she and her relations liven up a hallowe'en party to the delight of the children and the alarm of the local dignitaries. With a witch for a friend, Simon discovers, life is never dull.

Very highly recommended by ILEA's *Contact* magazine: '. . . who could resist such a lively character?'

You will find more adventures of Simon and the Witch in *The Return of the Witch*, *The Witch of Monopoly Manor* and *The Witch on Holiday*, all in Young Lions.